STICKER ENCYCLOPEDIA

DINOSAURS

DK | Penguin Random House

REVISED EDITION
Project Editor Olivia Stanford
Editor Radhika Haswani
Designers Charlotte Jennings, Jaileen Kaur
Senior Designer Nidhi Mehra
US Senior Editor Shannon Beatty
US Editor Elizabeth Searcy
Managing Editors Laura Gilbert, Alka Thakur Hazarika
Managing Art Editors Diane Peyton Jones, Romi Chakraborty
DTP Designer Dheeraj Singh
Picture Researcher Aditya Katyal
Jacket Designer Sonny Flynn
Pre-Production Producer Sophie Chatellier
Producer Basia Ossowska
Delhi Team Head Malavika Talukder
Creative Director Helen Senior
Publishing Director Sarah Larter

Subject Consultant Dr. Darren Naish

ORIGINAL EDITION
Written by Dougal Dixon
Edited by Sarah Davis
US Editor Margaret Parrish
Designed by Chloe Luxford
Jacket Designer Chloe Luxford
Design Assistants Wendy Bartlet, Fiona Gowen, Polly Appleton
Picture Research Chloe Luxford, Kate Lockley
Illustration by Peter Bull
Globes supplied by DK Cartography
Design Development Manager Helen Senior
Publishing Manager Becky Hunter
Associate Publisher Sue Leonard
Production Editor Andy Hilliard
Production Man Fai Lau

This American Edition, 2019
First American Edition, 2009
Published in the United States by DK Publishing,
a division of Penguin Random House LLC
1745 Broadway, 20th Floor, New York, NY 10019

Copyright © 2009, 2019 Dorling Kindersley Limited
24 25 26 16 15
023–312729–May/2019

All rights reserved.
Without limiting the rights under the copyright reserved above, no part of this publication may be reproduced, stored in or introduced into a retrieval system, or transmitted, in any form, or by any means (electronic, mechanical, photocopying, recording, or otherwise), without the prior written permission of the copyright owner.
Published in Great Britain by Dorling Kindersley Limited.

A catalog record for this book is available from the Library of Congress.
ISBN 978-1-4654-8148-1

DK books are available at special discounts when purchased in bulk for sales promotions, premiums, fund-raising, or educational use. For details, contact: DK Publishing Special Markets, 1745 Broadway, 20th Floor, New York, NY 10019
SpecialSales@dk.com

Printed and bound in China

www.dk.com

DK would like to thank Katie Lawrence for proofreading and Abigail Luscombe for editorial assistance and proofreading.

The publisher would like to thank the following for their kind permission to reproduce their photographs:
(Key: a-above; b-below/bottom; c-center; f-far; l-left; r-right; t-top)

1 Dorling Kindersley: Jon Hughes/Bedrock Studios (c); Jonathan Hately - modelmaker (cl). **4 Dorling Kindersley**: David Donkin - modelmaker (crb, c); Graham High at Centaur Studios - modelmaker (br, cr); Robert L. Braun - modelmaker (crb). **5 Dorling Kindersley**: Gary Staab - modelmaker (cr). **4–5** Luis Rey - modelmaker (b); **7 Dorling Kindersley**: Gary Staab - modelmaker (bl). **8–9 Dreamstime.com**: Martin Maun. **12–13 Dreamstime.com**: Selenka. **15 Dorling Kindersley**: Robert L. Braun - modelmaker (c); Natural History Museum, London (bc); Jeremy Hunt at Centaur Studios - modelmaker (ftr); Graham High at Centaur Studios - modelmaker (cra). **16–17 Dreamstime.com**: Iulianna Est. **18 Dreamstime.com**: Iulianna Est (background). **20 Dorling Kindersley**: Royal Tyrrell Museum of Palaeontology, Alberta, Canada (bl); **Dreamstime.com**: Iulianna Est (background). **21 Dorling Kindersley**: Centaur Studios - modelmakers (crb). **22–23 Dreamstime.com**: Jared Bauman. **24 Dorling Kindersley**: Jeremy Hunt at Centaur Studios - modelmaker (cl). **25 Dreamstime.com**: Cnaene (background). **26 Getty Images**: Altrendo Nature (cb); CGIBackgrounds.com (cb); Digital Vision / Sylvester Adams (clb); Bruno Morandi (b); Taxi / Michael Duva (cr). **27 Dorling Kindersley**: Centaur Studios - modelmakers (tr). **Getty Images**: Visuals Unlimited / Ken Lucas (bl). **28 Dreamstime.com**: Jared Bauman (background). **29 Dreamstime.com**: Tanwalai Silp Aran (background). **30–31 Dreamstime.com**: Mishoo. **32 Dreamstime.com**: Rangizzz (background). **33 Dreamstime.com**: Seadam (background). **35 Corbis**: Louie Psihoyos (tr, br). **38–39 Dreamstime.com**: Iulianna Est. **40 Dreamstime.com**: Seadam (background). **41 Dorling Kindersley**: Natural History Museum, London (c). **42–43 Dreamstime.com**: Martin Maun. **44 Dorling Kindersley**: Robert L. Braun - modelmaker (fcl); Dennis Wilson - modelmaker (cr); Natural History Museum, London (fbl). **45 Corbis**: Louie Psihoyos (tc); **Dorling Kindersley**: Natural History Museum, London (cla); Peabody Museum of Natural History, Yale University (cra). **46 Alamy Stock Photo**: YAY Media AS (b). **Dreamstime.com**: Mansum008 (background). **47 Dorling Kindersley**: Robert L. Braun - modelmaker (br). **48–49 Dreamstime.com**: Selenka. **49 Alamy Stock Photo**: Stocktrek Images, Inc. (cr). **52–53 Dreamstime.com**: Christopher Ewing. **54 Corbis**: Louie Psihoyos (bl). Dorling Kindersley: State Museum of Nature, Stuttgart (cla). **54–55 Dorling Kindersley**: Royal Tyrrell Museum of Palaeontology, Alberta, Canada. **56–57 Getty Images**: Altrendo Nature (lake). **58–59 Getty Images**: CGIBackgrounds.com (woodland). **60–61 Getty Images**: Taxi / Michael Duva (riverside forest). **62–63 Getty Images**: Digital Vision / Sylvester Adams (desert). **64–65 Getty Images**: Bruno Morandi (sea). **66 Corbis**: Louie Psihoyos (c/Allosaurus Tooth). **Dorling Kindersley**: The Natural History Museum (crb/Tooth); Jon Hughes (tr/Eoraptor); Royal Tyrrell Museum of Palaeontology, Alberta, Canada (cra/Ornitholestes); The Natural History Museum, London (cl/Tyrannosaurus Rex Skull); American Museum of Natural History (clb). **Science Photo Library**: Jaime Chirinos (cl/Troodon). **67 Dorling Kindersley**: The Natural History Museum (cb/Heterodontosaurus); Naturmuseum Senckenburg, Frankfurt (c, cb); The Natural History Museum, London (bc); Jon Hughes (ca). James Kuether: (bl). The Trustees of the Natural History Museum, London: Anness Publishing (cla). **70 Corbis**: Louie Psihoyos (fclb). **Dorling Kindersley**: John Holmes - modelmaker / Natural History Museum; The Natural History Museum, London (tl, cla/Nest, cb, cb/Iguandon Toe). **Getty Images**: National Geographic / O. Louis Mazzatenta (cra); Spencer Platt (cr); National Geographic / Ira Block (br). **71 Dorling Kindersley**: Gary Ombler / Robert L. Braun - modelmaker (cl); The Natural History Museum, London (tc, ca, cr); Royal Tyrrell Museum of Palaeontology, Alberta, Canada (cla/Maiasaura); Hunterian Museum University of Glasgow (clb/Cryptoclidus); Jon Hughes (cb). **Getty Images**: National Geographic / Jonathan S. Blair (crb). James Kuether: (clb). **74 Dorling Kindersley**: Sedgwick Museum of Geology, Cambridge (clb); Courtesy of Dorset Dinosaur Museum (ca/Eggs); Jon Hughes (crb/Peteinosaurus); Royal Tyrrell Museum of Palaeontology, Alberta, Canada (br); The Natural History Museum, London (bc). **Getty Images**: (cra); National Geographic / Jeffrey L. Osborn (tc); National Geographic / O. Louis Mazzatenta (ca, fcrb). **75 Dorling Kindersley**: Robert L. Braun (cla); The Natural History Museum, London (ca, tr, cr, crb/Skull); Jon Hughes (cra, crb); Senckenberg Nature Museum, Frankfurt (bc). **78 Alamy Stock Photo**: Oleksiy Maksymenko (clb). **Dorling Kindersley**: Jon Hughes (ca, cb); The Natural History Museum, London (tl, tc, cla/Skull, c, bc/Claw, br); Royal Tyrrell Museum of Palaeontology, Alberta, Canada (cl). **Getty Images**: National Geographic / Jeffrey L. Osborn (cla). James Kuether: (tr). **79 Alamy Stock Photo**: Stocktrek Images, Inc. (cla); YAY Media AS (cl). **Dorling Kindersley**: Tim Ridley / Robert L. Braun (ca/Herrerasaurus, ca); Royal Tyrrell Museum of Palaeontology, Alberta, Canada (tc, clb, crb/Ornithomimus); The Natural History Museum, London (crb). Getty Images: Mario Tama (c). **82 Dorling Kindersley**: Andy Crawford / Roby Braun (cra/Lesothosaurus); The Natural History Museum, London (cb/Baryonyx Claw, crb/Triceratops Skull, fbl/Stegosaurus Spike, br/Stegosaurus). **83 Dorling Kindersley**: Robert L. Braun (bc/Quadrupedal); The Natural History Museum, London (tr/Iguanodon Teeth, cra/Protoceratops, tc/Stegosaurus Spike, ca/Iguandon Footprint, fcra/Chirostenotes Claw, clb/Psittacosaurus, fcrb/Baryonyx Claw, crb/Iguandon Foot); Jon Hughes (cra/Eoraptor Lunensis). **Getty Images**: (cl/Nothronychus); National Geographic / Jeffrey L. Osborn (ftl/Masiakasaurus). **Science Photo Library**: Jaime Chirinos (crb). The Trustees of the Natural History Museum, London: Anness Publishing (tc/Torvosaurus). **86 Corbis**: Louie Psihoyos (crb/Allosaurus Tooth). Dorling Kindersley: Jon Hughes (Parasuchus, cl/Liopleurodon); The Natural History Museum, London (ftl/Chirostenotes Claw, cla/Pterodactylus, cla/Iguandon, cr/Stegosaurus Spike, cra/Baryonyx Skull, ca, fcla, fcl/Stegosaurus Spike, fcra, cb). Getty Images: National Geographic / O. Louis Mazzatenta (crb). **87 Dorling Kindersley**: John Holmes - modelmaker / Natural History Museum (clb/Nest); Hunterian Museum University of Glasgow (ca); Jon Hughes (cla/Anurognathus, fcrb); The Natural History Museum, London (fcla, cra/Triceratops Skull, fcla/Nest, cl, fcr, fcra/Skull, fcra/Psittacosaurus, fbr, bl). Getty Images: National Geographic / O. Louis Mazzatenta (fcl); Spencer Platt (tc); National Geographic / Jeffrey L. Osborn (bc). **90 Alamy Stock Photo**: Stocktrek Images, Inc. (fcra). Corbis: Louie Psihoyos (ftr). **Dorling Kindersley**: The Natural History Museum (bl); Jon Hughes (fcla/Liopleurodon, fcl/Anurognathus); The Natural History Museum, London (cra/Tooth, cla/Claw, ca/Skull, fcra/Chirostenotes Claw, fcl, cl, fcrb/Tooth, cb/Claw); Tim Ridley / Robert L. Braun (clb/Styracosaurus); Royal Tyrrell Museum of Palaeontology, Alberta, Canada (crb). **Getty Images**: National Geographic / Jeffrey L. Osborn (fcla). James Kuether: (tc, br). **Science Photo Library**: Jaime Chirinos (cb). **91 Alamy Stock Photo**: YAY Media AS (fcrb). **Dorling Kindersley**: The Natural History Museum (cb); Jon Hughes (tc, tr/Pterodaustro, fcla/Eudimorphodon, c, br); Courtesy of Dorset Dinosaur Museum (fcla); The Natural History Museum, London (ftr, cla/Nest, fcra, cb/Pterodactylus, cr/Spike, cb/Fossil); Tim Ridley / Robert L. Braun (cr); Hunterian Museum University of Glasgow (fcl); Andy Crawford / Roby Braun (cb/Lesothosaurus); Robert L. Braun (crb/Stegosaurus). James Kuether: (fcr, bc). **94 Corbis**: Louie Psihoyos (cla/Tooth, clb/Fossil). **Dorling Kindersley**: John Holmes - modelmaker / Natural History Museum (tr/Nest); Robert L. Braun (bc/Quadrupedal); Royal Tyrrell Museum of Palaeontology, Alberta, Canada (fbl/Skull, tc/Skull2, ca/Maiasaura, crb/Fossil); Jon Hughes (cb/Liopleurodon); The Natural History Museum, London (tc/Psittacosaurus, bc/Psittacosaurus, tr/Iguanodon Teeth, c, ftl/Iguanodon Teeth, cla/Skull, bc/Ginkgo, tc/Foot, bl/Fossil, bl/Footprint, crb/Footprint, tc, tc/Fossil, crb/Foot, fcrb/Claw, ca/Claw, cl/Foot, cl/Diplodocus, ca/Skull, cb/Archaeopteryx, cb/Shell, ca/Shell, fclb/Nest, cb/Albertosaurus, ca/Tooth, cra/Claw, Baryonyx, ca/Dawn Bird, clb/Protoceratops, fcra/Protoceratops, cla/Plates, fcrb/Head); Peabody Museum of Natural History, Yale University (cb/Foot Bones); State Museum of Nature, Stuttgart (fcr/Fossil); Courtesy of Dorset Dinosaur Museum (cr/Ichthyosaur). Getty Images: National Geographic / O. Louis Mazzatenta (tc/Skull); National Geographic / Jeffrey L. Osborn (ftr, clb, cra/Masiakasaurus, clb/Masiakasaurus, cb, c/Skeleton); National Geographic / Jonathan S. Blair (fcl/Skeleton); National Geographic / Ira Block (fcla); Spencer Platt (clb/Fossils). **Science Photo Library**: Jaime Chirinos (ftl). **95 Alamy Stock Photo**: Stocktrek Images, Inc. (fbl, fbr). **Corbis**: Louie Psihoyos (Tooth, crb/Tooth, tr). **Dorling Kindersley:** John Holmes - modelmaker / Natural History Museum (cl/Nest); The American Museum of Natural History (crb/Skeleton); The Natural History Museum, London (cl/Psittacosaurus, cr/Psittacosaurus, c/Iguanodon Teeth, crb/Skull, cl/Ginkgo, cla/Foot, bc/Foot, cb/Fossil, cra/Fossil, cla/Fossil, cr, fcr/Foot, clb/Claw, clb/Skull, tl/Archaeopteryx, fcra/Shell, tc/Nest, crb/Tooth2, crb, cra/Baryonyx, clb/Dawn Bird, tc/Protoceratops, cb, crb/Plates, cra/Footprint, tc/Head, cra/Skull); Royal Tyrrell Museum of Palaeontology, Alberta, Canada (c/Skull, ca/Fossil, fclb, cra/Skull2); Peabody Museum of Natural History, Yale University (fcla/Foot Bones); Jon Hughes (fcla/Liopleurodon, tl/Eudimorphodon); Courtesy of Dorset Dinosaur Museum (bc). **Getty Images**: National Geographic / O. Louis Mazzatenta (cl/Skull); National Geographic / Jeffrey L. Osborn (cra, c); National Geographic / Jonathan S. Blair (crb/Skeleton2); National Geographic / Ira Block (cb/Fossil2); Spencer Platt (cra/Fossils). James Kuether: (fcla)

Cover images: *Front and Back*: **Dreamstime.com**: Heike Falkenberg / Dslrpix (background); *Front*: **123RF.com**: ammit bc; **Dorling Kindersley**: Gary Ombler / Robert L. Braun cla, Courtesy of Dorset Dinosaur Museum bl; **Dreamstime.com**: Juliengrondin ca; *Spine*: **Dorling Kindersley**: The Natural History Museum, London t

All other images © Dorling Kindersley

About this book

HOW TO USE THIS BOOK

Read the information pages and then search for the relevant stickers at the back of the book to fill in the gaps. Use the sticker outlines and labels to help you.

There are lots of extra stickers that you can use to decorate the scenes at the back of the book. It's up to you where you put them all. The most important thing is to have lots of sticker fun!

PRONUNCIATION GUIDE

Dinosaur names can be long and tricky to say. Below many of the dinosaurs' names here you will see a pronunciation guide, for example, Shuvuuia (shoe-VOO-ee-ah). These break down each name into parts. The parts in capital letters should be said a little louder.

MIX
Paper | Supporting responsible forestry
FSC™ C018179
FSC www.fsc.org

This book was made with Forest Stewardship Council™ certified paper—one small step in DK's commitment to a sustainable future.
Learn more at
www.dk.com/uk/information/sustainability

Contents

The age of dinosaurs

Earth formed about 4.6 billion years ago. Experts have divided the passage of time since into chunks called eras. The dinosaurs lived in the Mesozoic era, which is broken up into the Triassic, Jurassic, and Cretaceous periods. Dinosaurs died out 66 million years ago (mya)—except for birds, which are descended from them.

DID YOU KNOW?
The colors of the sticker spaces in this book will tell you which period each animal lived in: red for Triassic, green for Jurassic, and yellow for Cretaceous.

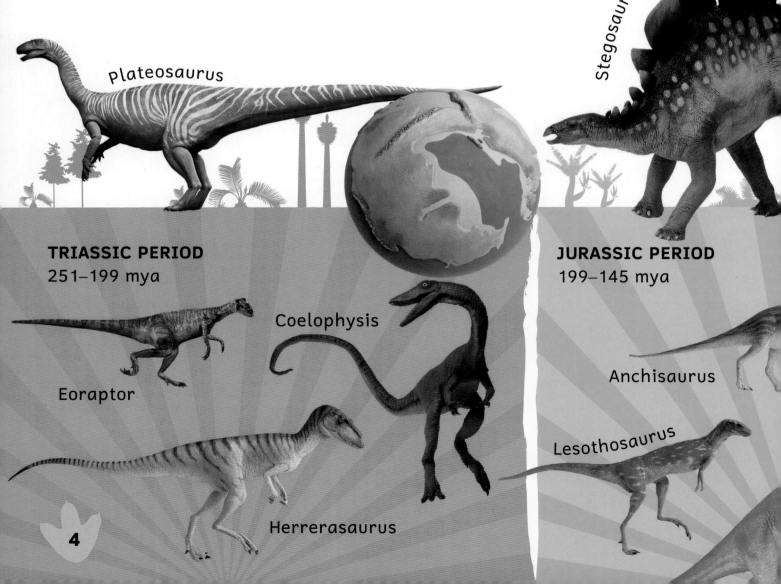

Plateosaurus

Stegosaurus

TRIASSIC PERIOD
251–199 mya

Coelophysis

Eoraptor

Herrerasaurus

JURASSIC PERIOD
199–145 mya

Anchisaurus

Lesothosaurus

4

What makes a dinosaur?

They all have scaly skin (some have feathers, too), long tails (used for balance and defense), legs that are held straight under the body, and claws.

Tyrannosaurus

CRETACEOUS PERIOD
145–66 mya

Giganotosaurus

Edmontonia

Velociraptor

Brachiosaurus

5

Small carnivores

Not all meat-eating dinosaurs were the enormous, terrifying type that killed the big plant eaters of the time. Some, like these, were very small and fed on smaller animals. But with their sharp teeth and claws they were still vicious.

FACT!

When Compsognathus was found in 1861, experts originally thought it was too small to be a dinosaur.

Shuvuuia
shoe-VOO-ee-ah
The strange thing about Shuvuuia was its forelimbs. They were short and stubby and ended in a single, clawed digit. It may have used this claw to dig into ants' nests.

Deinonychus
dye-noh-NIGH-kuss
With sickle-shaped claws on each foot, this predator could stand on one foot and slash at prey with the other.

Coelophysis
SEE-low-FI-sis
Coelophysis was a long and slender fox-sized hunter, feeding on small animals. It lived in family groups in the desert in Late Triassic or Early Jurassic times.

Eoraptor
EE-oh-RAP-tor
At a time when most of the world was desert, the dinosaurs evolved. Eoraptor ("dawn hunter") was one of the earliest. It lived in one of the few forests.

Ornitholestes
or–NITH–oh–LESS–tees

This dinosaur gets its name, "bird robber," from its long grasping hands. It lived in the riverside forests of Jurassic North America.

DID YOU KNOW?
Small dinosaurs were more intelligent than large ones.

Troodon
TRUE–oh–don

Turkey-sized Troodon is thought to have been one of the most intelligent dinosaurs of the Cretaceous woodlands. With its big eyes and sharp claws, it may have hunted, owllike, in the evenings.

Sinornithosaurus
si–NOR–nith–oh–SAW–russ

We know this dinosaur from very well-preserved skeletons, which even show its feathers. Its sharp teeth and claws show it to have been a fierce hunter. It lived along the banks of Chinese lakes.

Compsognathus
KOMP–soh–NATH–uss

This little dinosaur was about the size of a chicken. Only two skeletons of Compsognathus have been found, one with a lizard's bones in its stomach. It lived along Europe's seacoast in the Jurassic period.

Large carnivores

When we think of dinosaurs, we usually imagine the big, ferocious meat eaters featured here. These famous beasts lived in different places at different times, but they all fed on the other dinosaurs existing alongside them.

DID YOU KNOW?
The original skeleton of Spinosaurus was lost when its museum was bombed during World War II.

Dilophosaurus
dye–LOW–foh–SAW–russ
This dinosaur from the Early Jurassic deserts was about 20 ft (6 m) long. It carried two distinctive crests on its head—probably for showing off.

Ceratosaurus
se–RAT–oh–SAW–russ
Ceratosaurus looked like a dragon, with a nose horn and jagged crest. It hunted in the riverside forests of the Jurassic period.

Spinosaurus
SPINE–oh–SAW–russ
Spinosaurus lived in Africa in the Late Cretaceous period. The tall sail on its back may have been brightly colored and used for display.

8

Learn more on page 10.

Tyrannosaurus
tie-RAN-oh-SAW-russ
With its huge slashing teeth, Tyrannosaurus was one of the last of the meat eaters, prowling the woodlands of the Cretaceous period.

Concavenator
KON-ka-VEN-a-tour
This large predator stalked ancient Spain. It had a tall, narrow sail on its back, which might have been brightly colored and used in showing off to mates and rivals.

Giganotosaurus
gi-GAN-oh-toh-SAW-russ
This cousin of Allosaurus may have been the longest meat eater that ever lived and could have swallowed you whole. It lived in South America in the Late Cretaceous period. It was as heavy as an African elephant.

FACT!
Small meat eaters may have hunted in packs—big ones hunted alone.

Torvosaurus
torv-uh-SAW-russ
Torvosaurus was one of the biggest hunters in the Jurassic riverside forests—even bigger than its neighbor Allosaurus.

Learn more on page 11.

Allosaurus
a-low-SAW-russ
With its big clawed hands and its strong teeth, Allosaurus was the fiercest hunter in the Jurassic riverside forests. It was as heavy as a hippo.

Tyrannosaurus
tie–RAN–oh–SAW–russ

This is the most famous of the big meat-eating dinosaurs. With its enormous jaws and powerful teeth, it killed and ate the biggest plant eaters of the time. It probably hid in the bushes and ambushed prey, bursting out and smashing into it with the full weight of its body.

FACT FILE

Lived: 67–66 mya
Habitat: Woodland
Diet: Meat
Length: 39 ft (12 m)
Weight: 7 tons
(6.5 metric tons)
Name means: Tyrant lizard

Fossil finds

North America

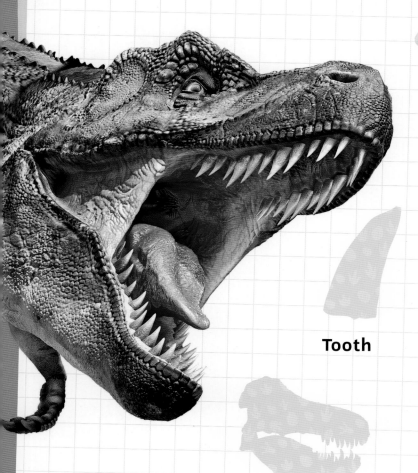

Tooth

Skull

Skeleton

In 1915, the first Tyrannosaurus skeleton was mounted for public view in New York's American Museum of Natural History. Pieced together from the bones of three partial skeletons, it was standing upright like a kangaroo instead of horizontally.

Allosaurus
a-low-SAW-russ

Allosaurus was the biggest of the meat eaters at the end of the Jurassic period. Unlike the later Tyrannosaurus, it had big strong arms with three huge claws on its fingers. It also had sharp claws on its feet.

FACT FILE

Lived: 150–145 mya
Habitat: Riverside forest
Diet: Meat
Length: 39 ft (12 m)
Weight: 2–3 tons
(1.8–2.7 metric tons)
Name means: Different lizard

Adult and baby tooth

Feeding frenzy
Allosaurus used its claws and teeth to rip flesh from other dinosaurs.

Fossil finds

Europe and Africa

North America

Skull
The skull of Allosaurus, like that of most dinosaurs, was full of holes and just made up of narrow strips of bone. This kept the weight of the head down and made it so flexible that it could gulp down huge chunks of meat. The teeth kept growing and dropping out when worn. They were replaced all the time by new ones.

Skeleton

Footprints
These tracks show Allosaurus and Apatosaurus footprints.

Other carnivores

There were many medium-sized meat-eating dinosaurs in the Triassic, Jurassic, and Cretaceous periods. Many other kinds of meat-eating animals lived there, too.

Xiongguanlong
jhi-ong-GOO-an-long

This Chinese dinosaur had an especially long, narrow snout. It was a big predator with a dangerous bite.

Rutiodon
ROOT-ee-uh-don

Although Rutiodon looked like a crocodile, it belonged to a group called the phytosaurs that was only distantly related. It prowled the desert streams of Triassic times.

Elaphrosaurus
ee-LAFF-ro-SAW-russ

This agile, wolf-sized dinosaur was one of the medium-sized carnivores of the Jurassic riverside forests.

DID YOU KNOW?
A few of the medium-sized meat-eating dinosaurs were as intelligent as some of today's birds.

Tanycolagreus
tan-ee-coh-LAG-ree-us

A little smaller than its neighbor Elaphrosaurus, Tanycolagreus dodged between the feet of the great plant eaters and hunted through the forest undergrowth.

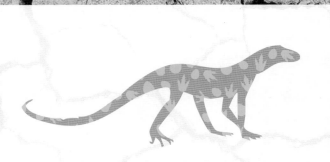

Terrestrisuchus
ter-rest-ree-SOOK-us

The earliest relatives of crocodiles were not like modern water dwellers. Terrestrisuchus, with its long legs, ran after small prey in the Triassic deserts.

Postosuchus
POST-uh-sook-uss

In the Triassic deserts, when the dinosaurs were first appearing, the main hunters were early relatives of crocodiles. Some, like Postosuchus, were as big as lions.

Fruitachampsa
froot-a-KAMP-sa

Fruitachampsa, another distant relative of crocodiles, lived in the riverside forests of the Jurassic period. It was the size of a cat and hunted lizards and small mammals.

FACT!

Most meat-eating animals just before the dinosaurs were crocodile relatives.

Piatnitzkysaurus
pee-at-NITS-kee-SAW-russ

This fast-moving meat eater lived in South America in Middle Jurassic times. It was not the biggest of the meat eaters but could tackle the young of the big plant-eating dinosaurs.

Food

Different dinosaurs ate different kinds of food. The earliest dinosaurs probably ate both small animals as well as plants. Many later types only ate plants, feeding on ferns and trees. The later meat eaters grew bigger and fed on the plant eaters. It was a savage world!

Monkey puzzle
This early tree was eaten by vegetarian dinosaurs.

FACT!

Discoveries of fossilized dung show that mighty Tyrannosaurus ate horned dinosaurs.

PLANT EATER

Iguanodon had a multipurpose hand. It walked on its three middle fingers. Its thumb was a spike for tearing down branches. The fifth finger could curl around to grasp food.

Dinosaur dung
We can learn a lot about the diets of dinosaurs and other ancient animals by looking at what is in their fossilized dung. Fossil dung is called a coprolite.

FISHING FOR FOOD

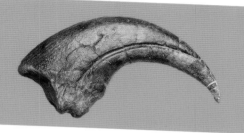

Some dinosaurs ate fish. Baryonyx gets its name, "heavy claw," from this huge, hooklike claw on its thumb. It stood by the river and hooked fish out of the water, like grizzly bears do today.

High-rise

Some long-necked dinosaurs, like Brachiosaurus, could lift their heads high into trees to reach the best leaves.

BUILT TO HUNT

The shape of a meat-eating dinosaur—long jaws, sharp teeth, running legs, claws—made it ideal for hunting and killing the animals on which it fed.

Ginkgo

This tree exists today, but fossils tell us that it dates back to dinosaur times. Many plant-eating dinosaurs fed on its fan-shaped leaves.

Small vegetarians

With so many different types of plants living at the time of the dinosaurs, it is not surprising that there were all kinds of dinosaurs that fed on them. Big dinosaurs usually ate food from high up in the trees, but small dinosaurs ate plants closer to the ground.

Cerasinops
seh-ra-SIN-ops
Cerasinops was a badger-sized relative of the big horned dinosaurs and, like them, lived in the woodlands at the end of the Cretaceous period.

Psittacosaurus
si-tak-a-SAW-russ
This dinosaur gets its name, "parrot lizard," from the huge beak in the front of its jaws. It used this beak to break into tough plants.

Scutellosaurus
skoo-tell-a-SAW-russ
Rows of armor plates ran along the sides and top of this small, plant-eating dinosaur. It was an early relative of the much larger Ankylosaurus and Stegosaurus.

Incisivosaurus
IN-sigh-seev-oh-SAW-russ
Its big front teeth made Incisivosaurus look a little like a rabbit. Otherwise, it looked like a turkey. It would have used the teeth to feed on lakeshore vegetation.

Heterodontosaurus
HET-er-oh-DON-toe-SAW-russ
Turkey-sized Heterodontosaurus had three different types of teeth—cutting teeth, chisel-like teeth, and sharp tusks—all useful for feeding on sparse desert vegetation.

Dryosaurus
DRY-oh-SAW-russ
Dryosaurus lived in the woodlands of what is now North America, Africa, and Europe. Its horny beak, at the front of the lower jaw, met with a toothless beak on the upper jaw. It was used for biting the tops off plants.

Stegoceras
STEG-oh-SEH-russ
Stegoceras had a thick bony skull and perhaps used it in head-butting battles with others of its herd, just as goats do today. Its teeth were great for shredding woodland undergrowth plants.

DID YOU KNOW?
Small plant-eating dinosaurs had teeth like vegetable graters, for ripping up plants.

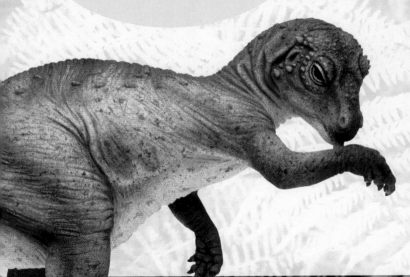

Thecodontosaurus
THEE-koh-DONT-oh-SAW-russ
Thecodontosaurus was the size of a large dog and it lived in the deserts of the Triassic period. It had a small head, long neck and tail, and saw-edged teeth. It was capable of walking on all four limbs.

More plant eaters

There were lots of different kinds of medium-sized plant-eating dinosaurs. Some of them belonged to the long-necked plant-eating group, and some of them belonged to the duckbill group (see p. 20).

(see p. 20)

DID YOU KNOW?
Dinosaurs existed for about a hundred times longer than humans have been on Earth.

Ouranosaurus
oo–RAN–oh–SAW–russ
Ouranosaurus was an amazing-looking animal! It had a big sail down its back and tail. The sail was used to keep it cool in the desert heat.

Massospondylus
MASS–oh–SPOND–ee–luss
This dinosaur was like Anchisaurus, but lived in Africa. It had a big claw (left) on its forefoot and used this to pull down leaves and branches from trees.

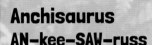

Learn more on page 19.

Anchisaurus
AN–kee–SAW–russ
Anchisaurus was one of the smaller long-necked plant eaters. It lived in the deserts of Triassic times and could rear up on its hind legs to feed from the trees in oases.

Maiasaura
MY–a–SAW–ra
Herds of this dinosaur nested together. We know this because experts have found their nests and babies in a site in Montana.

Maiasaura
MY-a-SAW-ra

The best-known dinosaur nests were made by the duckbill Maiasaura. These were found in the 1980s and show how dinosaurs brought up their youngsters.

FACT FILE

Lived: 80–74 mya
Habitat: Coastal plains
Diet: Leaves
Length: 30 ft (9 m)
Weight: 5½ tons
(5 metric tons)
Name means: Good earth-mother lizard

Skeleton

Egg nest

Infant

Fossil finds

North America

Good parents

The nests of Maiasaura were made of mud and soil formed into a pile, with branches and leaves placed on top. When the youngsters hatched, the parents brought them food and looked after them. When they were big enough, they migrated with the herd to the feeding grounds.

Fossil nest
This is a nest of baby duckbill dinosaurs found in the Gobi Desert in Asia.

Large vegetarians

Toward the end of the dinosaur age, the main plant eaters were large vegetarians called duckbills. These dinosaurs had mouths that were broad and flat at the front, but at the back there were lots of strong grinding teeth for dealing with tough vegetation.

DID YOU KNOW?
Lambeosaurus had more than 1,000 teeth—all for chewing plants.

Parasaurolophus
pa–ra–saw–roh–LOAF–uss
The crest on this dinosaur was used for making noises like a trombone, as it signaled to other dinosaurs in the woodlands where it lived.

Lambeosaurus
LAM–bee–oh–SAW–russ
Lambeosaurus was the same shape as Parasaurolophus. The hollow bony crests of these dinosaurs were used to attract mates and repel rivals.

Learn more on page 21.

Corythosaurus
ko–rith–oh–SAW–russ
The crest of this duckbill was semicircular and looked a little like an ancient Greek helmet. It lived in the woodlands of the Late Cretaceous period.

Iguanodon
ig–WAH–noh–don
Iguanodon lived at an earlier time than the duck-billed dinosaurs on this page and may have been their ancestor.

Iguanodon
ig-WAH-noh-don

Iguanodon was discovered in the 1820s. At first, only the fossil teeth—obviously belonging to a plant eater—were found. The only plant-eating reptile known at that time was the iguana lizard, and so the fossil animal was named Iguanodon.

FACT FILE

Lived: 135–125 mya
Habitat: Lake
Diet: Plants
Length: 30 ft (9 m)
Weight: 4½–5½ tons (4–5 metric tons)
Name means: Iguana tooth

Fossil finds

Europe

Teeth

Skull

Footprints

In the 1870s a whole herd of complete Iguanodon skeletons was found in Belgium, Europe. People could see for the first time what the whole animal was like. Since then, remains—including footprints—have been found all over the world.

Giant vegetarians

The long-necked plant-eating dinosaurs were the biggest land animals that ever lived. They were the most important plant eaters in the first half of the age of dinosaurs. Later, they became less common in some areas and were replaced by the duckbills.

Patagotitan
pat–AG–oh–tie–tan

One of the biggest of the giant vegetarians, Patagotitan was longer than 115 ft (35 m). It lived in South America alongside some especially big meat-eating dinosaurs.

Amargasaurus
a–MAR–ga–SAW–russ

This strange vegetarian from South America had a double row of long spines along its neck and a fin down its back. It probably used these to show off.

Barosaurus
BA–roh–SAW–russ

This had one of the longest necks of any dinosaur. It could sweep its tiny head around like the hose of a vacuum cleaner and collect food from a wide area.

Camarasaurus
KAM–ar–oh–SAW–russ

From North America, this dinosaur was the most common of the giant plant eaters of the Jurassic riverside forests. Its skull was distinctively short and boxlike, and it had huge nostrils.

Apatosaurus
a-PAT-oh-SAW-russ

Apatosaurus is one of the best known giant vegetarians from the riverside forests of the Jurassic period. It was closely related to its cousin Brontosaurus.

Diplodocus
di-ploh-DOKE-uss

Diplodocus used its incredibly long tail as a whip to keep enemies away. Along with Barosaurus and Apatosaurus, it fed on the low vegetation of the riverside forests.

Brachiosaurus
brak-KEY-oh-SAW-russ

Brachiosaurus lived at the same time as Apatosaurus, but whereas Apatosaurus fed from low-growing vegetation, Brachiosaurus, with its tall shoulders and long neck, ate from the tops of the trees.

Dreadnoughtus
dred-NOT-tuss

This gigantic, long-necked plant eater lived in what is now Argentina. The neck of Dreadnoughtus was unusually long, making up about half of its total length.

DID YOU KNOW?
Some plant eaters swallowed stones to help them grind up their food.

23

Diplodocus
di-ploh-DOKE-uss

Diplodocus is one of the longest of the known dinosaurs. Despite its length it was quite lightweight. Its long neck enabled it to reach out for food over a wide area, and its long tail was used like a whip.

FACT FILE

Lived: 155–145 mya
Habitat: Riverside forest
Diet: Leaves
Length: 89 ft (27 m)
Weight: 13 tons (12 metric tons)
Name means: Double beam

Fossil finds

North America

Skeleton

We know a lot about Diplodocus from the many skeletons found. The head has narrow jaws with comblike teeth—it just raked up its food and swallowed, without chewing. Its tail bones had skid-like structures beneath them, to protect the tail if it dragged on the ground. The backbones were full of air spaces, to keep the skeleton light.

Backbone

Tail skid

24

Other vegetarians

It was not just the dinosaurs that ate the plants of the Triassic, Jurassic, and Cretaceous periods. All kinds of other animals lived in those times as well, and many competed with them for food.

Macelognathus
mass-el-og-NATH-uss
This cat-sized animal was actually a kind of long-legged plant-eating relative of crocodiles. It had broad shovel-shaped jaws and ate leaves from the ground plants of the Jurassic forests.

Placerias
pla-SEER-ee-uss
Placerias lived in the oases of the Triassic deserts. Its long tusks helped it dig up roots, and its turtle-like beak could break off tough stems.

Proganochelys
PRO-gan-uh-kee-lees
Turtles are a very old group of animals. They date back to animals like Proganochelys that lived in the deserts of Triassic times. They had shells like modern turtles.

Desmatosuchus
dez-mat-oh-SOO-kuss
In the Triassic deserts there lived animals that were related to crocodiles. Desmatosuchus, with its spiked shoulders and its piglike head, fed from low-growing plants.

Habitats

The dinosaurs' world was very different from ours. There were no cities or fields or roads, in fact, nothing built by people. Mountains and seas were in different places, creating totally different landscapes. Even the plants were different—flowers appeared only at the very end of dinosaur times.

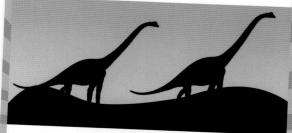

MIGRATION

Some dinosaurs, like other animals, migrated every year to find food or to reach their nesting sites as the seasons changed. These journeys would have been dangerous.

Where dinosaurs roamed

A habitat is an area that animals and plants share, for example, seas, deserts, lakes, woodlands, and riverside forests.

Lake

Riverside forest

Desert

Woodland

Sea

LANDSCAPES

In early dinosaur times the plants were all green and brown, with no real flowers. In the Cretaceous period, flowers like magnolias and buttercups appeared. The last dinosaurs lived in a colorful world.

CAMOUFLAGE

Some big plant eaters were probably colored green and brown. They could hide from meat eaters among the plants of the forests.

Fossilized fern
Before grasses appeared, ferns covered much of the ground during the age of dinosaurs.

FACT!

Grass did not evolve until very late in dinosaur times. There were no grassy plains habitats.

Home, sweet home
Gallimimus lived on open plains.

Tree dwellers

Some of the smallest dinosaurs could climb trees. We can tell this because fossils have been found with long toes and curved claws, like those of modern tree-dwelling birds.

Archaeopteryx
AHR-kee-OP-ter-iks
Archaeopteryx was one of the first birds. It evolved from dinosaurs that climbed trees. It developed wings with flight feathers that helped it fly from tree to tree.

Microraptor
MY-crow-RAP-tor
This was the smallest nonbird dinosaur known. It lived by lakes, and the feathers on its arms and legs allowed it to glide from tree to tree.

Scansoriopteryx
scan-sore-ee-OP-ter-IKS
Scansoriopteryx was another tiny dinosaur. It may have had primitive wings that would have allowed it to glide. Like Microraptor, it lived around the lakes of Early Cretaceous China.

Epidendrosaurus
ep-EE-den-dro-SAW-russ
The long fingers (above) and toes of Epidendrosaurus show that it climbed trees, alongside its relatives Microraptor and Scansoriopteryx.

In the sky

A group of flying reptiles called pterosaurs lived alongside dinosaurs but were only distantly related to them. They had small furry bodies and broad leathery wings.

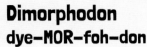

Dimorphodon
dye-MOR-foh-don

This pterosaur had a deep head and a long tail. Like the others, Dimorphodon had a furry body and leathery wings.

Eudimorphodon
YOU-dye-MORF-oh-don

Pterosaurs appeared at the same time as the first dinosaurs. Eudimorphodon was one of the earliest.

FACT!

Dimorphodon means "two-form teeth." It had some big and some small ones.

Icarosaurus
IK-ah-ro-SAW-russ

Before the pterosaurs evolved, lizard-like animals like Icarosaurus glided across the rocky crags of the Triassic deserts.

Anurognathus
ann-uh-rog-NATH-uss

This was one of the smallest of the pterosaurs. About the size of a gull, it hunted insects through the Jurassic woods and forests.

In the sky

The pterosaurs varied as much as modern birds do—some were tiny and others were massive. The wings were made of skin supported on a very long fourth finger that was as strong as the arm.

Pterodactylus
teh-ra-DACT-a-luss

Pterodactylus lived in the same time and place as Rhamphorhynchus, but it was less primitive. This and all the later pterosaurs had short tails.

Peteinosaurus
pe-TEEN-uh-SAW-russ

This was one of the earliest pterosaurs and flew above the deserts of Triassic times. Like other primitive types, such as Rhamphorhynchus, it had a long stiff tail.

Criorhynchus
cry-oh-RINK-uss

Criorhynchus was a large pterosaur, with a wingspan like an albatross. It soared over the ocean in Cretaceous times.

Quetzalcoatlus
ket-zal-KWAT-luss

One of the biggest pterosaurs known is Quetzalcoatlus. It flew above the woodlands of Late Cretaceous North America.

DID YOU KNOW?
Quetzalcoatlus was the size of a small airplane.

Sinopterus
sine-OP-ter-us
About the size of a pigeon, Sinopterus fed on insects and plant material from the trees that overhung the lakes of Early Cretaceous China.

FACT!
At first, scientists thought that pterosaurs must be swimming animals— they couldn't believe they could fly.

Pterodaustro
teh-ra-DOW-strow
This pterosaur was similar to a flamingo. Its jaws were armed with brushlike bristles, and it filtered tiny animals from lakes and lagoons, just like flamingos do.

Rhamphorhynchus
ram-for-RINK-uss
Rhamphorhynchus had long toothy jaws and a long stiff tail. A diamond-shaped fin at the end of its tail may have been used for display.

Nyctosaurus
NIK-toe-saw-russ
This strange pterosaur lived in the air above the oceans at the end of the Cretaceous period. It had a bony crest on its head that was three times as long as the skull itself.

Sea reptiles

When the dinosaurs were the rulers of the land, there were all kinds of strange reptiles that lived in the sea. Some of these were as big and fierce as the dinosaurs themselves.

Ichthyosaurus
ik-thee-oh-SAW-russ

The name Ichthyosaurus means "fish-lizard" and describes it perfectly. Even though it was a reptile, it had a fishlike body and tail, a fin on its back, and its limbs were swimming paddles.

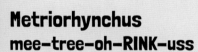

Metriorhynchus
mee-tree-oh-RINK-uss

Some distant relatives of modern crocodiles became seagoing animals. Metriorhynchus was so well adapted to a swimming way of life that it had a fishlike tail fin and flippers for limbs.

Cryptoclidus
crip-toe-CLIDE-uss

Related to the pliosaurs, the plesiosaurs were long-necked fish-eating reptiles with little heads and sharp teeth. Cryptoclidus was a typical plesiosaur.

Liopleurodon
lie-oh-PLEUR-uh-don

Liopleurodon belonged to a group of huge swimming reptiles called the pliosaurs. They cruised the oceans hunting for prey. Their limbs evolved into winglike flippers, like the wings of penguins.

FACT!

The fossils of sea-dwelling animals are more common than those of land dwellers like dinosaurs.

Freshwater reptiles

A whole range of swimming reptiles lived in the rivers and lakes of dinosaur times. These were mostly much smaller than their dinosaur relatives, but some were real giants.

Tanytrachelos
tan–ee–TRAK–el–os
This long-necked reptile lived in the ponds and desert streams of the Triassic period, swimming with its strong tail and long hind legs, feeding on insects and other small animals.

Hyphalosaurus
hi–FAL–oh–saw–russ
This reptile was like a lizard with a long neck. It used its webbed feet for swimming in the lakes of Cretaceous China.

DID YOU KNOW?
All land animals evolved from water animals. Some, like those shown here, returned to the water.

Deinosuchus
dye–noh–SOO–kuss
This was the biggest member of the crocodile family that ever lived. It existed at the end of the Cretaceous period and ate dinosaurs that came to the rivers to drink.

Champsosaurus
kamp–so–SAW–russ
Although Champsosaurus looked like a crocodile, it was only distantly related. It lived in Cretaceous rivers and snapped up fish with its long jaws.

Eggs, nests, and young

All dinosaurs laid eggs, and some built nests like birds. The baby developed in the egg until it was ready to hatch. Dinosaur eggs had hard shells, but some reptile eggs—such as those of the flying pterosaurs—had leathery shells, similar to the eggs of snakes and lizards.

CITIPATI EGG

Citipati nests found in Mongolia show that the eggs were laid in a spiral. Each egg was about 6 in (16 cm) long.

Citipati nest
Like modern birds, Citipati spread its feathered body over its eggs to warm them.

JUST HATCHED

Most dinosaurs, after hatching, could walk and look after themselves. The parents would look after them, bringing them food and defending them, until they were big enough to leave the nest.

FOSSILIZED NEST

It is hard to match dinosaurs to particular fossil eggs. These, from Montana, were thought to have been laid by a plant-eating dinosaur. Now experts believe they are from a meat eater.

FACT!

The biggest dinosaur egg ever found—18 in (46 cm) long—was laid by a long-necked plant eater.

Tiny baby

This newly hatched Mussaurus ("mouse lizard") is one of the smallest nonbird dinosaurs ever found. It emerged from a 1 in (2.5 cm) long egg, and the adult would have been 10 ft (3 m) long.

Feathered

A few perfectly fossilized skeletons show that at least some small dinosaurs were covered in feathers. The feathers were not for flying, but for warmth.

DID YOU KNOW?
The claws of Therizinosaurus were about 35 in (90 cm) long—about the size of a person's arm.

Dromaeosaurus
DROH—mee—oh—SAW—russ
The name means "running lizard," and this active hunter was related to Velociraptor, hunting small animals in the woodlands of North America.

Epidexipteryx
ep—EE—dex—ip—TER—ix
This small chicken-sized meat eater, from Chinese woodlands and forests, had an unusual arrangement of plumes on its tail.

Therizinosaurus
theh—ra—ZEE—NA—SAW—russ
This strange animal was related to the meat eaters but was a plant eater. It used its big claws to pull branches down from trees.

Sinosauropteryx
SINE-oh-SAW-ROP-ter-IKS
We can actually see the feathers on the fossil of Sinosauropteryx, since it was preserved in mud at the bottom of a lake in the Early Cretaceous period.

Velociraptor
ve-LOSS-ee-RAP-tor
Velociraptor was about the size of a turkey. It was a desert-dwelling predator that most likely hunted smaller dinosaurs as well as lizards and other prey.

Citipati
SI-tee-PA-tee
We know this dinosaur from many skeletons, one of which has been found sitting on eggs in a nest. This is one of its eggs.

FACT!
Different dinosaurs had different types of feathers. Some had feathers like modern birds, while others had simpler hairlike strands.

Caudipteryx
kaw-DIP-ter-iks
Caudipteryx had fanlike bunches of feathers on its arms and tail. It used these to signal to other animals on the lake banks.

Nothronychus
NOTH-ro-nike-uss
This was a smaller relative of Therizinosaurus and lived in the woodlands of Late Cretaceous North America. It also had long claws and ate leaves.

Fur and feathers

Mammals and birds were around during the time of the dinosaurs. The birds brightened up the landscape with their colorful plumage, but the mammals were probably mostly hidden, camouflaged by their mousy-colored fur.

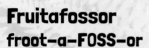

Fruitafossor
froot–a–FOSS–or
Burrowing into the riverbanks of the Jurassic forests, Fruitafossor kept out of the way of the big dinosaurs and hunted worms and burrowing insects.

Oligokyphus
O–lig–oh–ky–fuss
Mammals evolved from a group of animals called synapsids. Some of these, like Oligokyphus, looked just like mammals but were reptilelike in some features of their skeleton.

DID YOU KNOW?
Three-quarters of all types of birds and mammals became extinct along with the nonbird dinosaurs.

Yanornis
yan–OR–nis
Most birds that lived around the Early Cretaceous lakes showed a mixture of bird features and dinosaur features. The size of a pigeon, Yanornis was probably the ancestor of modern birds, but it had teeth in its jaws.

Schowalteria
show-wal-ter-EE-a

In the woodlands of the very end of the age of dinosaurs lived mammals like Schowalteria, ready to take over as soon as the dinosaurs disappeared.

Hesperornis
hes-per-OR-niss

The bones of this bird show that it was a flightless sea dweller, swimming after fish like a modern penguin. It lived among the great sea reptiles of the end of the Cretaceous period.

FACT!

The first mammals appeared at the same time as the first dinosaurs.

Confuciusornis
con-FYOOSH-ee-SOR-niss

If you saw Confuciusornis flying over the lakes of Cretaceous China, you would think it was a modern bird, with long tail feathers. But it had dinosaur-like claws on its wings.

Cimolestes
sigh-moh-LESS-tees

Rat-sized Cimolestes fed on insects in the woodland trees at the end of the Cretaceous period. It survived into the beginning of the age of mammals, once the dinosaurs became extinct.

Repenomamus
rep-en-OH-mam-uss

Most mammals during dinosaur times were tiny—about mouse sized. Repenomamus was much bigger—about the size of a badger—and it ate baby dinosaurs.

Fish eaters

During dinosaur times, rivers and lakes were full of fish. Some dinosaurs evolved to hunt these. Experts can identify fish-eating animals by their teeth and claws, which are perfect for catching slippery prey. Fossilized fish bones have also been found in their stomachs.

Learn more on page 41.

DID YOU KNOW?
Most modern seabirds eat fish. It is not surprising, therefore, that some of their ancestors, the dinosaurs, did too.

Baryonyx
barry–ON–iks
Baryonyx lived in the marshes of the Early Cretaceous period. It had an unusual crocodile-shaped skull, and its huge, curved thumb claw—about 12 in (30 cm) long—was ideal for catching fish.

Suchomimus
SOO–koh–MIME–uss
Suchomimus was like a large version of Baryonyx, but with a low sail down its back. It lived in Africa at the same time as Baryonyx lived in Europe.

Parasuchus
PA–ruh–sook–uss
Parasuchus was neither a dinosaur nor a crocodile—it belonged to a group called the phytosaurs. Like a crocodile, it lived in water and hunted fish in Triassic times.

Masiakasaurus
MA–she–ka–SAW–russ
The fossils of this dinosaur were found in Madagascar. The teeth at the front of the mouth were ideal for snapping up fish from rivers.

Baryonyx
ba-REE-ON-iks

Discovered in the 1980s, Baryonyx was the first fish-eating dinosaur known. Although it was well adapted to catching and eating fish, it did eat other things as well. Parts of Iguanodon bones were found in its stomach along with fish scales.

FACT FILE

Lived: 125 mya
Habitat: Riverbanks
Diet: Fish
Length: 33 ft (10 m)
Weight: 2 tons
(2 metric tons)
Name means: Heavy claw

Fossil finds

Europe

Skeleton

Everything about the skeleton of Baryonyx tells us that it was a fishing animal. The jaws were long and narrow, like those of a fish-eating crocodile. The many teeth were small and pointed—ideal for catching and holding slippery prey—and the huge hooklike claw on its thumb would have been used for snatching fish out of the water.

Skull

Foot

Claw

Fast runners

Small meat-eating dinosaurs were fast runners. They had to be to catch their food. And, of course, most of the small plant-eating dinosaurs had to be fast runners, too—so that they could escape them.

Lesothosaurus
leh–SOH–toe–SAW–russ
This was one of the earliest two-footed plant eaters. It was no bigger than a large lizard and lived in the African deserts.

Hypsilophodon
hip–si–LOW–foh–don
Called the "gazelle of the dinosaur world," Hypsilophodon had strong running legs to help it escape the big meat eaters that lived in Europe at the beginning of the Cretaceous period.

Ornithomimus
or–NITH–oh–MY–muss
Ornithomimus was not only the size of an ostrich, but it also looked like one. With its long legs, it dodged between woodland trees and sprinted across plains.

FACT!
The smallest dinosaur footprints ever discovered came from a dinosaur as small as a sparrow.

Gallimimus
gal-i-MY-muss

Gallimimus was a long-legged runner, related to Ornithomimus and Struthiomimus. It was a little larger than the other two and lived in Asia rather than North America.

DID YOU KNOW?
Gallimimus, Ornithomimus, and Struthiomimus could all run about as fast as a racehorse.

Struthiomimus
STREW-thee-oh-MY-muss

Like its neighbor Ornithomimus, Struthiomimus was like an ostrich. They both lived in North America in Late Cretaceous times.

Chindesaurus
CHIN-dee-SAW-russ

Most of the meat-eating dinosaurs of the Early Jurassic deserts were small, fast-running animals. Like Chindesaurus, they could chase their prey over rocks and dry sand.

Herrerasaurus
heh-RARE-ra-SAW-russ

Pony-sized Herrerasaurus was one of the earliest meat eaters from the deserts of South America. It chased smaller dinosaurs and other reptiles.

Hunting and defense

In the animal world, plant eaters eat the plants, and meat eaters eat the plant eaters. It was the same in dinosaur times. Some of the meat-eating dinosaurs were such ferocious hunters that the plant eaters evolved all kinds of body weaponry in order to protect themselves.

FACT!

Giganotosaurus may have slammed into its victims to knock them out with its body weight, before eating them.

ARMORED

Gastonia was built like a tank and covered in bony studs for armor. Wicked spikes jutted out from its sides and its shoulders to keep fierce meat eaters away.

Tall tails
Some dinosaur tails were used as weapons.

Stegosaurus had long spikes on the end of its tail for jabbing at predators.

Euoplocephalus had a club of fused bone at the end of its tail to swing at predators.

Diplodocus used its long tail as a whip.

Locked in battle

These skeletons of Velociraptor and Protoceratops are fossilized together. They fought each other to the death.

KILLER CLAW

Deinonychus, or "terrible claw," got its name from the killer claw on the second toe of each foot. They were used to slash at prey.

WARNING SIGNALS

If in danger, Parasaurolophus could use its long crest—made from its nose bones—as a trumpet to make noises to warn the herd.

Allosaurus

This terrifying predator had special joints in its jaw that enabled it to open its mouth extra wide and gulp down the flesh of its victims.

Plated dinosaurs

Some plant-eating dinosaurs had plates on their backs instead of armor. These plates may have been used as weapons, or they may have been for showing off. Most of them lived in the Late Jurassic and Early Cretaceous periods.

DID YOU KNOW?
The plates on dinosaurs were not attached to their skeletons—just embedded in the skin.

Learn more on page 47.

Stegosaurus
STEG–oh–SAW–russ

Stegosaurus is the biggest and best known of the plated dinosaurs. It lived in the riverside forests of Late Jurassic North America.

Miragaia
mih–ruh–GUY–ah

What made this dinosaur unusual was its long, flexible neck. It could have fed from the ground as well as high up from trees and bushes.

Dacentrurus
DASS–en–true–russ

Dacentrurus had small plates over the back and neck, but long spikelike plates over the hips and tail. It lived in Europe in Jurassic times.

Gigantspinosaurus
gi–GANT–spine–uh–SAW–russ

As its name suggests, this dinosaur had gigantic spines. They swept sideways from the shoulders like great wings and were used as defense against the meat eaters of the Chinese plains.

Stegosaurus
STEG-oh-SAW-russ

Stegosaurus had a double row of plates down its back, some of them rounded and some pointed. At the end of its tail it carried two pairs of spikes for defense. Its head was long and narrow, with jaws ideal for grabbing leaves and fruit.

FACT FILE

Lived: 155–144 mya
Habitat: Riverside forest
Diet: Plants
Length: 20 ft (6 m)
Weight: 2 tons
(2 metric tons)
Name means: Roof lizard

Fossil finds

Europe   North America

Tooth

Plate fossil

Tail spike

Skeleton

Dozens of Stegosaurus skeletons exist, and from these we can tell that the plates were made of bony slabs covered in horn. The tail spikes were sharp weapons covered in horn, which Stegosaurus used to swing at enemies. The teeth had coarse serrations on them for shredding plants.

Horned dinosaurs

The horned dinosaurs had different numbers of horns arranged in different patterns on their heads. These animals used their horns and bony frills for fighting and sending signals to each other.

DID YOU KNOW?
The earliest horned dinosaurs lived in Asia. The later ones lived only in North America.

Styracosaurus
sty–RACK–oh–SAW–russ
You would always be able to recognize Styracosaurus, because of the long spikes that jutted out from the back of its neck frill. It had a single horn on its nose.

Hongshanosaurus
hong–shan–oh–SAW–russ
This was one of the earliest horned dinosaurs. It lived by the lakes of Early Cretaceous China.

Chasmosaurus
kaz–moh–SAW–russ
This horned dinosaur had an extremely long frill. It would have been brightly colored like a flag and used for showing off to other dinosaurs in the Cretaceous woodlands.

Learn more
on page 50.

Aquilops
a–KWIL–ops

The narrow, curved beak of this
small horned dinosaur explains its
name, which means "eagle face."
It lived in the western United States
and was less than 2 ft (60 cm) long.

Protoceratops
PROH–toh–SEH–RA–tops

This was a desert-dwelling dinosaur
that took shelter in large burrows that
it dug with its hands and feet.

Albertaceratops
al–BURT–a–SEH–RA–tops

Scientists keep finding new
species of horned dinosaur.
Albertaceratops is one of the
new ones—named only in 2007.

FACT!

The dinosaur horns
mentioned here were
like those of cows—bony
cores covered in horn.

Leptoceratops
lep-toe-SEH–RA-tops

Leptoceratops, the size of
a small sheep, was one of
the small primitive horned
dinosaurs. It lived in the
Cretaceous woodlands
along with its big relatives.

Centrosaurus
SEN-troh-SAW-russ

Like Styracosaurus, also
from the Cretaceous woodlands,
Centrosaurus had a single big
horn on the nose. But it did not
have the long spikes around
the frill.

Lived: 85–80 mya
Habitat: Desert
Diet: Plants
Length: 6 ft (1.8 m)
Weight: 400 lb (180 kg)
Name means: Before the horned faces

Fossil finds

Asia

Protoceratops
PROH-toh-SEH-RA-tops

The earliest horned dinosaurs like Protoceratops were small rabbit- or sheep-sized animals. They did not actually have any horns, but their heads were heavy and had the neck shields and big beaks of their bigger relatives.

Infant skull

Adult skull

Complete skeleton
Scientists have found whole herds of Protoceratops skeletons in the Gobi Desert in Asia. Many of them were complete and had been preserved when they were buried in sandstorms. This area of central Asia was desert even in Cretaceous times.

Triceratops
try-SEH-RA-tops

At the end of the Cretaceous period, the horned dinosaurs became really big, and Triceratops was the biggest. It needed its neck shield and its three horns to show off to other Triceratops.

Fossil finds

North America

Skull

Horn

Horns and shields

Triceratops, just like the other horned dinosaurs, had horns pointing forward. When danger came, Triceratops always turned to face it. That way it could protect its body with its neck shield.

Armored

Many plant eaters evolved armor and horns to show each other how strong they were. Armor would also have helped protect them from big meat eaters, such as Tyrannosaurus.

Learn more on page 51.

Triceratops
try–SEH–RA–tops
This is the most famous and the biggest of the horned dinosaurs. It had three horns: two long ones above the eyes and a smaller one on the nose.

Ankylosaurus
an–KYE–low–SAW–russ
Ankylosaurus was armored like a tank. Its main weapon was a club on the end of its tail, made from heavy bone. The vertebrae of the tail were fused together to form a stiff shaft.

FACT!
The weak spot on armored dinosaurs was their underbelly.

Stygimoloch
STIJ–ee–moh–lok
In addition to a dome on its head for battering enemies, Stygimoloch had spikes all over its head. Like these other armored dinosaurs, it lived in the Late Cretaceous woodlands.

Euoplocephalus
YOU–oh–ploh–sef–a–luss
Euoplocephalus had a club on its stiff straight tail, like its relative Ankylosaurus. Also, its back was covered in horn-covered armor.

Edmontonia
ed–mon–TONE–ee–ah

Edmontonia had most of its weapons on its shoulders. Huge spikes stuck out sideways and forward, so that it could charge at its enemies. There were also spikes along its sides and tail.

Pentaceratops
pen–ta–SEH–RA–tops

Some dinosaurs had horns rather than armor. The horns were mounted on the head, and there was an armored frill protecting the neck. Pentaceratops had a huge frill that made its head look enormous.

Gastonia
ga–STONE–ee–ah

Gastonia's tail had a series of bladelike plates jutting sideways from it. As the tail curled, the plates slid over one another like scissor blades, cutting and injuring anything caught in between.

Sauropelta
SAW–ra–PELT–a

Sauropelta came earlier than the other armored dinosaurs on these two pages. Its main weapons were the rows of spikes on each side of the neck. Its back and long tail were also covered in armor.

Fossils and finds

Dinosaurs, except for birds, have been extinct for tens of millions of years. We know what they were like from the remains that have been found preserved in rocks. Mostly, their fossils are of isolated scraps of bone, but sometimes whole skeletons are preserved.

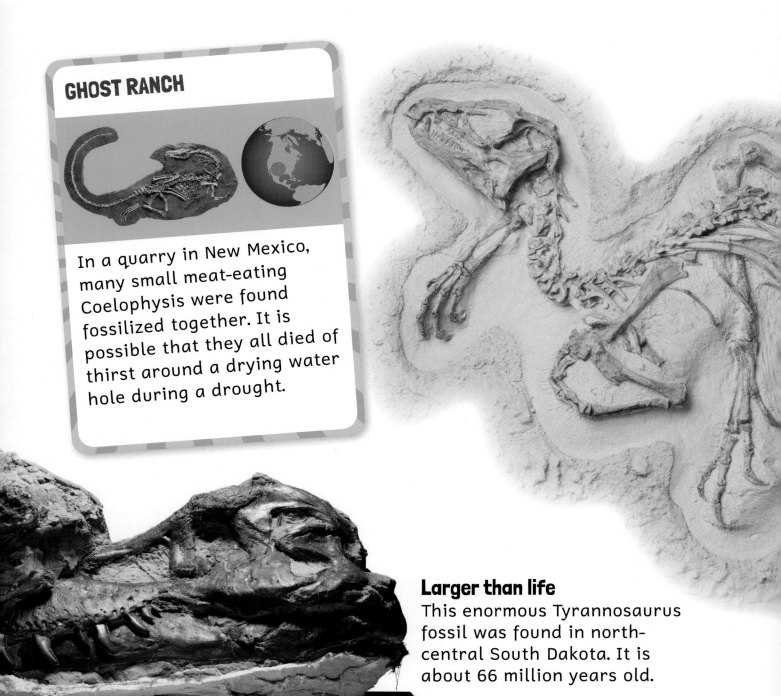

GHOST RANCH

In a quarry in New Mexico, many small meat-eating Coelophysis were found fossilized together. It is possible that they all died of thirst around a drying water hole during a drought.

Larger than life
This enormous Tyrannosaurus fossil was found in north-central South Dakota. It is about 66 million years old.

Ammonite fossil
Most fossils are of sea animals, like this ammonite. They were buried in seafloor mud and turned to rock.

DINOSAUR NATIONAL MONUMENT

Sometimes dinosaurs were washed down rivers and fossilized where the currents tumbled them together. This site in Utah has 1,500 dinosaur fossils in a layer of river sandstone.

Rare head
Dinosaur skulls do not often fossilize—they are too delicate. This Gallimimus skull is unusually complete.

Heterodontosaurus
This Heterodontosaurus fossil is well preserved and shows its whole skeleton.

FACT!
Fossil comes from the Latin word fossilis. It means "dug up."

Lake

CHECKLIST

Use the stickers in the book to fill up the scene. Here are some animals that you might find here. Which is your favorite?

- [ ] Sinopterus
- [ ] Hyphalosaurus
- [ ] Caudipteryx
- [ ] Sinornithosaurus
- [ ] Repenomamus

Woodland

CHECKLIST

Use the stickers in the book to fill up the scene. Here are some animals that you might find here. Which is your favorite?

- ☐ Tyrannosaurus
- ☐ Triceratops
- ☐ Troodon
- ☐ Ornithomimus
- ☐ Quetzalcoatlus
- ☐ Nothronychus
- ☐ Schowalteria

Riverside forest

CHECKLIST

Use the stickers in the book to fill up the scene. Here are some animals that you might find here. Which is your favorite?

- [ ] Fruitachampsa
- [ ] Allosaurus
- [ ] Elaphrosaurus
- [ ] Tanycolagreus
- [ ] Brachiosaurus
- [ ] Diplodocus
- [ ] Apatosaurus
- [ ] Champsosaurus
- [ ] Stegosaurus

Desert

CHECKLIST

Use the stickers in the book to fill up the scene. Here are some animals that you might find here. Which is your favorite?

- [ ] Coelophysis
- [ ] Dilophosaurus
- [ ] Rutiodon
- [ ] Anchisaurus
- [ ] Desmatosuchus
- [ ] Peteinosaurus
- [ ] Icarosaurus
- [ ] Oligokyphus
- [ ] Scutellosaurus

Sea

CHECKLIST

Use the stickers in the book to fill up the scene. Here are some animals that you might find here. Which is your favorite?

- [ ] Ichthyosaurus
- [ ] Liopleurodon
- [ ] Metriorhynchus
- [ ] Compsognathus
- [ ] Anurognathus
- [ ] Pterodactylus
- [ ] Rhamphorhynchus
- [ ] Dacentrurus

Deinonychus

Eoraptor

Shuvuuia

Sinornithosaurus

Ornitholestes

Troodon

Compsognathus

Coelophysis

Tyrannosaurus
skull

Allosaurus
teeth

Allosaurus and
Apatosaurus
footprints

Tyrannosaurus
tooth

Giganotosaurus

Allosaurus
skeleton

Rutiodon

Postosuchus

Icarosaurus

Tanycolagreus

Piatnitzkysaurus

Tyrannosaurus

Baryonyx foot

Concavenator

Ceratosaurus

Torvosaurus

Spinosaurus

Allosaurus

Tyrannosaurus

Dilophosaurus

Tyrannosaurus
skeleton

Allosaurus

Triceratops
skull

Fruitachampsa

Heterodontosaurus

Deinosuchus

Xiongguanlong

Diplodocus
skull

Elaphrosaurus

Psittacosaurus

Dryosaurus

Cerasinops

Thecodontosaurus

Incisivosaurus skull

Maiasaura nest

Scutellosaurus

Maiasaura nest

Microraptor fossil

Massospondylus claw

Fruitafossor

Iguanodon skull

Terrestrisuchus

Baby duckbill fossilized nest

Iguanodon footprint

Proganochelys skull

Iguanodon

Diplodocus

Maiasaura infant

Epidendrosaurus fingers

Stegoceras

Iguanodon teeth

Anchisaurus

Maiasaura skeleton

Iguanodon footprint

Parasaurolophus skeleton

Brachiosaurus

Diplodocus tail skid

Dimorphodon

Dreadnoughtus

Patagotitan

Camarasaurus

Cryptoclidus skeleton

Eudimorphodon

Placerias skeleton

Barosaurus

Corythosaurus

Amargasaurus

Velociraptor

Caudipteryx

Sinosauropteryx
fossil

Schowalteria

Citipati egg

Nothronychus

Therizinosaurus

Cimolestes

Repenomamus

Oligokyphus

Diplodocus

Confuciusornis
fossil

Criorhynchus

Ichthyosaurus

Peteinosaurus

Yanornis

Stegosaurus
tail spike

Dromaeosaurus
skeleton

Sinopterus

Champsosaurus

Hesperornis bone

Diplodocus backbone

Epidexipteryx

Anurognathus

Stegosaurus

Centrosaurus

Stegosaurus tooth

Struthiomimus

Suchomimus

Baryonyx skull

Scansoriopteryx

Hypsilophodon

Pterodaustro

Quetzalcoatlus

Stegosaurus skeleton

Pterodactylus

Archaeopteryx

Nyctosaurus

Protoceratops
infant skull

Protoceratops skeleton

Euoplocephalus

Masiakasaurus

Parasuchus

Protoceratops

Gigantspinosaurus

Protoceratops
adult skull

Triceratops
horn

Ankylosaurus
tail club

Liopleurodon

Chasmosaurus skeleton

Sauropelta

Baryonyx thumb claw

Pentaceratops

Stegosaurus
plate fossil

Gastonia

Lambeosaurus head

Metriorhynchus

Chindesaurus

Herrerasaurus

Edmontonia

Aquilops

Styracosaurus

Albertaceratops

Miragaia

Stygimoloch skull

Triceratops

Triceratops skeleton

Baryonyx fossil

Ornithomimus skeleton

Protoceratops

Triceratops

Leptoceratops

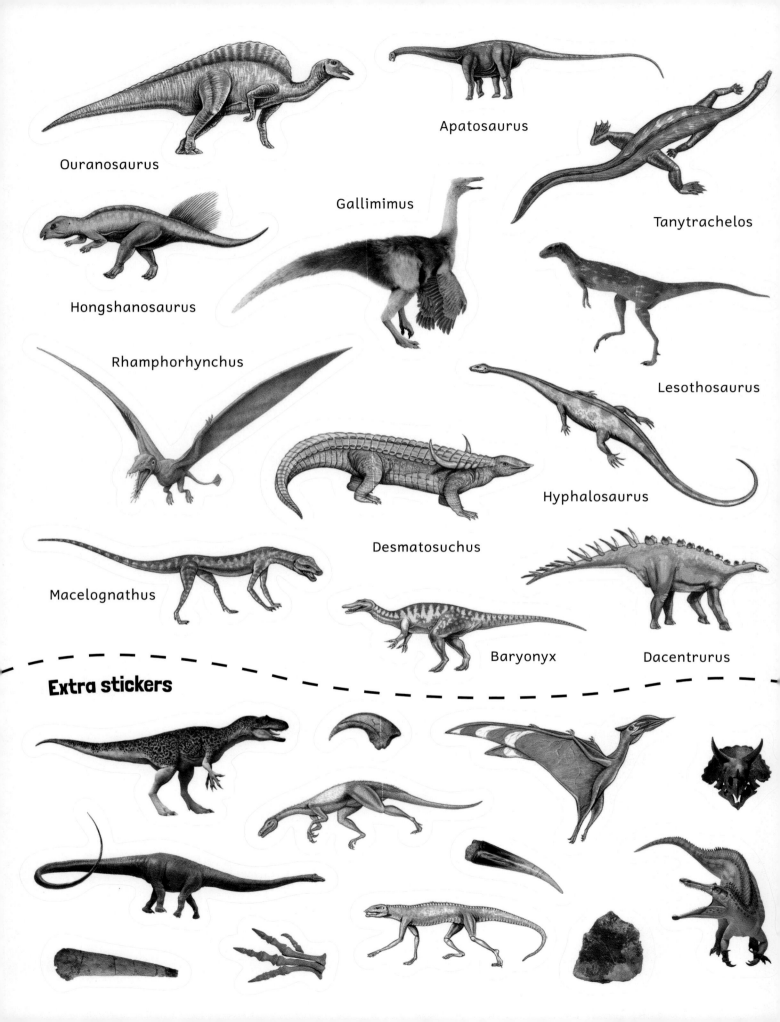

Ouranosaurus

Apatosaurus

Tanytrachelos

Gallimimus

Hongshanosaurus

Lesothosaurus

Rhamphorhynchus

Hyphalosaurus

Desmatosuchus

Macelognathus

Baryonyx

Dacentrurus

Extra stickers